CONTENTS

Introduction 4
Volume 1: 6
Going back to go forward 6
Survival 7
Rusks (Beskuit) 9
    Buttermilk rusks (Karringmelk beskuit) 12
    Aniseed rusks (Mosbeskuit) 13
First love – 14
Why I love to hate Red Bush (Rooibos) tea 14
    Rooibos (Red Bush) tea chocolate cake 17
    Rooibos (Red Bush) tea ganache-like icing 18
Fitting IN 19
Peppermint Crisp Tart 20
Easy-peasy chocolate cake 24
.... 24
Pancakes 27
    Simple 28
    Light and airy 29
Spice cake 30
Banana Bread 32
.... 32
Baked apple pudding 34
    Sauce 35
Malva Pudding 36
    Sauce 38
Volume two: 39
Heritage 39

Melktert	43
Koeksisters	46
Koeksisters dough	48
Syrup:	48
Cape Brandy Pudding	50
(Tipsy Tart)	50
Bread (Brood)	53
Farm loaf	54
Yoghurt loaf	55
Vetkoek	56
Plaatkoekies	59
All-purpose pastry	61
Savoury Muffins	62
Chemistry	65
CLEMENTINE Drizzle Cake	67
Carrot Cake	70
Drizzle Icing	73
Cream cheese icing	73
Apple cake	74
The next Volume:	77
to drink or not to drink Rooibos Tea	77
Rooibos Tea Fruiht Cake	79
Epilogue	81

M's Kitchen is a place of true intimacy where sense and soul meet and confidence has room to grow

- MARIANNA MARKS

The majority of the recipes shared in this book have been passed on to me by my grandmother. Some of the recipes have been shared by family or friends over the years. These have been adapted to suit our UK climate and ingredients. All are a celebration of the many cultural influences we share when enjoying Southern African baking

INTRODUCTION

"So what U doing"

"I'm naked baking and dancing..."

NINE WORDS AND A PAUSE.

Two lines of chat without the appropriate punctuation and we were entering the realms of an entirely different conversation.

The fact that I was moving in and out of my kitchen wearing a tangerine bikini top and black shorts seemed suddenly irrelevant.

I was floating – whether from the aromas of the Rooibos tea chocolate cake filling every corner of my kitchen, the effects of the sun on my skin or the possibility of new love after a difficult break-up; I felt different and my whole body was tingling with anticipation.

It was not always like this.

In an alternate world my time was split between trying to be supermom and helping organisations doing clever research or making innovative products find their own voice.

The sad fact was that I had lost mine.

Ask me what my favourite song of the moment was or which movie I enjoyed best in the last three or six months and I simply could not answer.

Who had time to think about movies or colours when the world and everything around you was changing so fast, you could only just about get through the day.

So, I stopped thinking about myself, what I cared about and just how tired I was.

Soon enough I felt all but invisible.

Worse still, given that I work in communications, I genuinely believed my voice no longer mattered.

It was in M's Kitchen - a room measuring just 12 square metres including all the fixtures and fittings, that I found myself again.

It was here that I came to process when things got tough, here where I simply could not block out my innermost thoughts and feelings.

In M's Kitchen is where I cried, here where I let go and mourned the loss of self. Here where I could see her breathing, the woman who used to laugh and flirt and love with all her heart.

To find her again, I had to mentally undress, accept that things would never be the same and get back to what mattered to me now.

I had to get naked with her in every sense of the word.

VOLUME 1:
GOING BACK TO GO FORWARD

SURVIVAL

WHEN YOU READ OR HEAR OF STORIES ABOUT WAR, POLITICAL CONFLICT OR PAINFUL DEATH, YOUR OWN PAIN AND ANXIETIES SEEM RATHER INSIGNIFICANT.

Thus, when Francois Willem crossed the street in 1972 to be knocked into the hereafter by a car, the earth did not in fact stop on its axis, there was no public outcry over safety or segment in the newspaper or on the radio. No balloons were let loose in the sky. Only the lives of the ones left behind changed forever.

For one side of my family, this is what I call triggering the cycle of survival.

The life paths altered for a young man with the same name – my dad, who witnessed his father killed right before his eyes.

A young bride – my mother, who knew he was dead before my dad had time to tell her and that formidable woman, Maria Anna, my grandmother - widowed too soon and left to care for four younger children in an era where men were expected to provide for their families.

What does this have to do with baking you might wonder?

In Southern Africa, stories of conflict, pain and survival are interwoven with food and family recipes.

Food dried or preserved to ensure survival during school term times or conscription, as a snack after full-body contact sports such as rugby or used simply to relieve hunger or quiet restless children during travel; food is seldom just food.

Food, especially baking, is personal.

A journey as it were through your family history, associated with your best or worst childhood memories and what you give when you want to please or impress.

My grandmother, like so many women faced with challenging times, baked well enough to inspire several generations.

It was her ability to bake the highest rising and incredibly moist chocolate cake I had ever tasted for our birthdays that first inspired me to try baking.

Admittedly it took me a while to get the technique right.

This was partly a combination of subconsciously fighting preconceived gender roles and the fact that my mother hardly ever baked.

My mother, a beautiful, petite woman with raven black hair and sapphire eyes, did not like us making a mess in her kitchen. I was no exception to this rule.

So, when I got my first job as a teenager, I bought my own ingredients, tested my baking on my friends and persevered.

Fortunately, until recently just before her death, I could always phone my gran to ask her how to get recipes to turn out like hers. The last time we chatted via my uncle, I asked her to tell me how to get koeksisters to properly absorb the syrup.

As she passes through to the hereafter, I am grateful to her for believing in M's Kitchen when I first moved to the UK and for sharing some of her recipes with me.

I also thank my aunts Susan and Hester for letting me have their recipes for tried and tested Malva and Apple Pudding. I have tested and adapted these recipes to suit our climate, my oven and style of baking.

I share these recipes and my food stories from M's Kitchen in these pages on my pathway to healing and lasting love.

RUSKS (BESKUIT)

NOTHING REMINDS ME OF PRECIOUS TIME WITH FAMILY MORE THAN BESKUIT (RUSKS) DIPPED INTO COFFEE OR TEA.

Please note I am not talking about the rusks you find in the UK used to wean babies – this recipe is for rusks that are super-snacks in their own right.

Rusks can be plain or filled to the brim with all sorts – seeds, nuts and/ or dried fruit and can keep you going for a few hours at least.

Whenever we travelled from Namibia to see family in South Africa (around a day's worth of driving), we would stop at the roadside, stretch our legs and have rusks with tea.

In those days we did have something resembling motorway services, but many families would use these to refuel or have a comfort break only.

Rusks were usually stored in a round plastic or metal cake tin. The smell that would hit you as soon as you carefully took off the lid, so as not to dent it or drop it, will stay with me always.

Originally, I am certain, rusks would have been a way to portion and dry loaves of bread to keep them from spoiling.

These days rusks are like cereal bars - available all year round and filled to the brim with so many delicious ingredients such as pumpkin seeds, sunflower seeds, coconut, apricot, aniseed, etc. You can easily have these for breakfast and are limited only by your imagination in how or where you eat them.

Personally, I like to bake rusks when the leaves start to colour and autumn sets in.

It allows me to take an almost magical mental carpet ride back home away from the reality of months of grey, wind and rain that lie ahead.

I also love to give these to those I care about to remind them of home.

My all-time favourite rusks must be the ones using my grandmother's buttermilk recipe.

I now regularly substitute some of the ingredients with those I have in my cupboard – pistachio nuts, goji-, acai- or cranberries, pumpkin seeds or hemp hearts.

Both types of rusks in the recipes below will last for months when stored in an airtight container.

BUTTERMILK RUSKS (KARRINGMELK BESKUIT)

Ingredients

2 kg self raising flour
750 grams butter
4 teaspoons (20 ml) baking powder
200 grams desiccated coconut
2 cups (500 ml) oats
30 grams bran flakes
½ packet (approximately 50 grams) sunflower seeds
4 cups (1 litre) sugar
6 large, free range eggs
4 cups (1 litre) buttermilk
2 teaspoons (10 ml) ground pink salt

Directions

- Pre-heat the oven to 165°C (180°C if not a convection fan oven)
- Melt the butter in a pan or in the microwave
- Whisk eggs and sugar together
- Add melted butter and buttermilk
- Mix dry ingredients together and add to the above mixture
- Transfer to a large deep baking or roasting tray
- Bake for approximately 60 minutes until brown
- Cool
- Cut into squares or rectangles, spread out on baking trays and dry out in the oven at around 100°C for 5-6 hours or until dry

ANISEED RUSKS (MOSBESKUIT)

Ingredients

125 grams margarine or butter
2 cups (500 ml) sugar
2 cups (500 ml) hot water
2 cups (500 ml) warm milk
3 large, free range eggs
10 grams dried yeast dissolved in 1/2 cup (125ml) lukewarm water
2 tablespoons (30 ml) honey
15 cups (around 2.5 kg) plain flour
2 teaspoons (10 ml) ground pink salt
2 tablespoons (30 ml) aniseed/ caraway seeds

Directions

- Preheat oven to 145°C if convection fan oven, otherwise 165°C
- Prepare baking tray or loaf pans with margarine or butter or cooking spray
- Mix the butter, sugar, water and milk
- Stir until the sugar dissolves and cool
- Add the eggs, yeast and honey and mix together with four cups of flour. Cover and rest until it starts to bubble on the top (The smell will tell you it is ready)
- Add the remaining flour, salt and aniseed/ caraway seeds to the sourdough mixture. Knead until elastic (stretchy in feel and does not stick to your hands – around 20 minutes)
- Cover and let it rise until double in size (this could be several hours in the UK winter)
- Knead lightly. Oil your hands, break off equal balls of dough and place in bread pans
- Let it rise until double in size
- Bake for 40-60 minutes until cooked (skewer comes out clean)
- Mix together 1 teaspoon (5 ml) sugar and 1 tablespoon (15 ml) warm milk. Brush over the bread as it comes out the oven. Bake for a couple more minutes
- Cool down and remove from tray/ pans. Break off and enjoy. This can also be dried out in the oven like the buttermilk rusks

FIRST LOVE –
WHY I LOVE TO HATE RED BUSH (ROOIBOS) TEA

ELEVEN O'CLOCK. THE TIME MY DAD FINISHED WORKING THE NIGHT SHIFT.

A typical toddler, I wanted to spend as much time with him as possible. The fly in the proverbial ointment was he seemed to work all the time.

So, I started waiting. Night after night I would wake up when he came home, banging my sippy-cup on the table, demanding that I needed to have tea with him.

Caffeine and sugary drinks were definite no-no's growing up in Namibia, so black, slightly-cooled Rooibos tea was the drink of choice for thousands of babies and toddlers like me.

From reducing colic, indigestion and used as a treatment for numerous skin ailments, the reported benefits of Rooibos are well documented.

For me Rooibos tea was a drink of affection – the special ritual I got to share with my dad.

Funny how the things you grow up with, you either love or hate when you are a grown-up.

To this day my love-hate relationship with Rooibos tea continues, but it is always a staple ingredient in my kitchen cupboard.

Ironically, it is the only tea that my mother asks me for when I do get to make tea for her.

The Rooibos tea "thing" also ended up as an extended family thing.

Starting what is believed to be the original Rooibos tea company in Clanwilliam – Eleven O'clock Rooibos tea, the Ginsburg family tree eventually merged with mine.

I have fond memories of hours of conversation with my now ex's grandfather about how they first discovered the tea, how they used to dry the tea on the warehouse floor, how he buried a diamond as big as a matchbox under a tree (not sure about how true this last one was), etc.

The tea that I had shared with my dad had become the story of my own nuclear family - even though my ex still does not drink Rooibos tea.

These days I very seldom get to share Rooibos tea with anyone.

However, the ritual and nostalgia of love and family becomes one and that special extra ingredient when I bake this Rooibos tea chocolate cake with a Rooibos tea ganache-like topping.

ROOIBOS (RED BUSH) TEA CHOCOLATE CAKE

Ingredients

1 cup (250 ml) hot water
2 - 3 Rooibos tea bags
5 large, free-range eggs, separated
1.75 cups (375 ml) castor sugar
½ cup (125 ml) sunflower/ canola oil
1 teaspoon (5 ml) vanilla extract/ bean paste
½ cup (125 ml) raw cocoa powder
2 cups (500 ml) plain flour
1 tablespoon (15 ml) baking powder
½ teaspoon (2.5 ml) ground pink salt

Directions

- Pre-heat the oven to 165°C (180°C if not a convection fan oven like mine)
- Prepare (line with baking parchment or use butter or a cooking spray) two cake tins (I use a silicone mold)
- Pour boiling water over the tea bags and leave to infuse for around 3-5 minutes
- Whisk the egg yolks and sugar together until light and fluffy
- Add the oil and vanilla extract
- Add the sieved cocoa powder to the tea (remember to remove the tea bags) and mix to a smooth paste
- Sift together the dry ingredients (flour, baking powder and salt)
- Add to the cocoa powder paste and mix thoroughly
- Beat the egg whites to soft peak stage (the ends flop over when you remove the whisk) and fold into the cocoa powder mixture
- Pour into the cake tins/ mold and bake for approximately 30-60 minutes depending on your oven (Use a skewer inserted into the centre of the cake to check)
- Cool down and turn out of the cake pans/ mold

ROOIBOS (RED BUSH) TEA GANACHE-LIKE ICING

Ingredients

2 cups (500 ml) hot water
2-3 Rooibos tea bags
1 cup (250 ml) castor sugar
¼ cup (62.5 ml) butter
¼ cup (62.5 ml) raw cocoa powder
¼ cup (62.5 ml) corn flour
1.5 teaspoons (7.5 ml) vanilla extract/ bean paste

Directions

- Pour boiling water over the tea bags and leave to infuse for 3-5 minutes
- Melt sugar and butter and over a low heat in a pan
- Mix corn flour with a little of the tea (remember to remove the tea bags), Add the cocoa and stir until smooth
- Add to the pan and mix well
- Heat on low heat and continue stirring until the mixture has thickened
- Add the vanilla extract/ paste
- Cool until set – this could take several hours
- Spread over the cake
- Decorate with flaked almonds/ macadamia nuts or edible berries of your choice

FITTING IN

FOURTEEN AND GOING ON 24; WE WERE UNSTOPPABLE.

For most of my teenage years my friend and I spent almost every day after school together.

My sister (and probably many like her) thought I was mixing with the wrong crowd.

Looking back, I realise we were mostly bored, in love with the idea of love and hungry given how much walking we used to do.

Usually on a Friday, we were (at least I was) baking at her house.

Although she was and still is substantially leaner than me, it is with her that I first discovered my love of making and giving food as gifts.

If you have heard of the Five Love Languages, you would certainly think my love language for showing love is through gifts.

Although I like to show rather than say I love you, my real love language is spending quality time together. Something I only really figured out later in life.

A sippy-cup of tea with my dad, coffee with a friend, a braai in my garden with friends or family; simple things, but vitally important to me.

I owe my friend Carol a thank you for letting me find out how I like to express and receive love and affection.

Love is and always will be a deed for me and none more so than when you give of yourself to someone you care about.

Although this recipe does not require baking, it is very much about fitting in, so I have included this here.

PEPPERMINT CRISP TART

Ingredients

1 pack (200 grams) Tennis biscuits (or use any biscuits you can find with coconut in it like Nice biscuits)
3 tablespoons (45 ml) melted butter
1 tin caramel condensed milk
1 tub double cream (250 ml)
Peppermint Crisp bar (or chocolate with mint) grated

Directions

- Prepare the dish using cooking spray or butter
- Crush the biscuits, mix with the melted butter or margarine and line the bottom of the tin
- Whisk the cream until thick and mix with the caramel
- Pour into the base
- Grate Peppermint Crisp over top and chill for about 3 hours or overnight

LATER, WHEN I BECAME A PARENT THE NEED TO FIT IN CAME FULL CIRCLE.

No matter how much planning I did, whether I worked from home or not, there always seemed to be a cake sale I did not have a plate for, a fundraiser or festival I was not aware of until the night before or on the day; the list goes on and on.

These days of course you can just go to the shop, but what do you do if you are stuck in the loop of trying to live up to your heritage and it is now 10 o'clock at night?

OK, let us take a quick step back.

When I was growing up, going to the shop never seemed like an acceptable option.

Moms baked. If you wanted to fit in, so did yours.

Unfortunately, my mom did not seem to share this same desire to bake.

She was quite happy being by herself and never appeared to get caught up in all the politics of trying to belong in a world where being an individual got you into trouble.

By the time I got to high school, the pressure to fit in became very real as you might be able to surmise from the previous story.

What is more, my mom was not someone who served on committees or had tea with her friends.

She stayed at home, went to church, expected me to do well at school and behave. How I achieved that was up to me, as long as I did just that.

Hence the parts of me that wanted to be social like my grandmother and OK with being an individual like my mother started to clash. As did my mother and I.

Why did I not just ask my grandmother to bake for me, you might ask.

Well, I did not really want to admit that my mother did not bake and competing for my grandmother's attention with her work, church, social and family commitments seemed somehow selfish.

Eventually my ability to earn my own money bought me some space and the possibility to make and bake what I wanted.

By the time I was in the final year of high school my grandmother had nearly a dozen grandchildren and what appeared like the social calendar of a political candidate.

Even though we shared a name and similar looks, I did not feel comfortable asking her to help me with my now weekly baking schedule.

Sadly, even though I improved quickly, I never really felt that my mom approved. Either of the mess I undoubtedly created or how much I was spending on baked goods that never remained in the house.

I guess independence comes at a price. So does trying to be great at baking.

Over the next few pages I share some of my tried and tested, easy bake and definitely "more please" recipes that get me through parties, school fairs and fundraisers year on year.

These recipes are what I call my last-minute bakes and should help if you find yourself having to supply baked goods at short notice or if you are looking to fit in just a little more.

EASY-PEASY CHOCOLATE CAKE

BY THE AGE OF EIGHT I THINK I HAD REALISED THAT IF YOU WANTED TO BAKE WELL, YOU HAD TO PRACTICE.

My grandmother, Maria Anna, was a home economics inspector for the Department of Education in Namibia and if that was not intimidating enough, she always seemed to make and bake the most amazing food, especially her high-rise chocolate cake.

I can still see her arriving at my school at break-time with my freshly baked birthday cake – massive, beautifully iced and decorated with Peppermint Crisp shavings.

This amazing woman's tough exterior scared me as a child, but now I completely understand how challenging it must have been to have primary responsibility for a family and still find time to bake and help raise funds for much needed causes.

This is not that birthday cake recipe, but it is one of the first recipes she shared with me when I moved to the UK.

This is a definite bake-me-when-you-are-in-a-hurry recipe and can be baked in a roasting tray (in her words the deep black one that comes standard with most ovens).

It contains coffee, which keeps it moist for up to two weeks if stored in a fridge, but there is no reason you cannot substitute the coffee with tea of your choice. Just remember to remove the tea bags/ strain the tea if using leaf tea.

Ingredients

Cake Mix:

1.75 cups (437.5 ml) plain flour
3 teaspoons (15 ml) baking powder
Pinch of ground pink salt
5 large eggs, separated and whites beaten to stiff-peak stage
1.5 cups (375 ml) castor sugar
¾ cup (187.5 ml) sunflower/ vegetable oil
3 tablespoons (45 ml) raw cocoa
¾ cup (187.5 ml) water

Sauce:

2.5 cups (625 ml) water
¼ cup (62.5 ml) castor sugar
3 tablespoons (45 ml) instant coffee powder

Directions

Cake:

- Preheat the oven to 165°C (180°C if you do not have a convection fan oven)
- Prepare (treat with margarine or butter or cooking spray) an oven roasting tray
- Sift together 1.75 cups (437.5 ml) flour, 3 teaspoons baking powder and salt
- Beat the egg yolks, sugar and oil together
- Add the cocoa powder
- Add the water and mix well
- Add the flour mixture and mix
- Fold in the egg whites
- Bake for approximate 25 minutes until cooked (skewer inserted into the middle comes out clean)

Sauce:

- Add to a pan and gently simmer the ingredients for around 10 minutes
- Pierce the cake with skewer and pour over the sauce to absorb faster
- You can ice this cake with a topping made from a mixture of one tin of caramel condensed milk and one cup (250ml) fresh cream whisked until thick

PANCAKES

PANCAKES ARE SO SIMPLE, YOU MIGHT BE FORGIVEN FOR ASKING WHY I HAVE INCLUDED THE RECIPE IN THIS BOOK.

Making the batter requires just a few minutes of your time, sure. But then resting the batter and having a light touch and knowing when to turn the pancakes, is one of those skills you would do well to develop. Much like knowing when and how to have a difficult conversation with a loved one.

SIMPLE

Ingredients

3 cups (750 ml) plain flour
2 teaspoon (10 ml) baking powder
2 tablespoon (30 ml) sunflower oil
3 teaspoons (15 ml) white vinegar
2 large, free-range eggs
4 cups (1 litre) lukewarm water

Directions

- Mix together all the ingredients until the batter is smooth and no lumps remain
- Rest the batter for 30 minutes and fry the pancakes in a pan coated with oil/ spray
- Serve with cinnamon and sugar or a topping of your choice

LIGHT AND AIRY

Ingredients

4 large, free-range eggs separated, whites whisked to stiff peak stage
2 cups (500 ml) water
2 cups (500 ml) semi-skimmed milk
¾ cup (185 ml) sunflower oil
3 cups (750 ml) plain flour
1 teaspoon (15 ml) baking powder
2 teaspoons (10 ml) ground pink salt
½ teaspoon (5 ml) ground nutmeg

Directions

- Beat eggs yolks together with the oil
- Add the liquid (milk and water)
- Add dry ingredients (flour, baking powder, salt, nutmeg)
- Fold in the egg whites
- Bake pancakes and sprinkle over some cinnamon and sugar or a topping of your choice and serve

SPICE CAKE

UNTIL I LIVED HERE, I NEVER REALLY VALUED A CAKE WITHOUT ICING. This cake is like the cakes you would find in the Mediterranean countries and was introduced to South Africa by the Greeks I believe. It has a caramel-like topping and is one of the few cakes I immediately want to taste as soon as it comes out of the oven. Given the fact that it does not have icing, you can keep this for several days in an airtight container. Somehow, I do not think you will have to worry about that. I often replace the spices with what I have in my cupboard, the key is if you like the taste of a spice, use it.

Ingredients

Cake Mix:
1 cup (250 ml) plain flour
Pinch (1 ml) ground pink salt
½ teaspoon (2.5 ml) mixed spices (you can use mixed herbs too)
1 teaspoon (5 ml) ground cinnamon
½ teaspoon 2.5 ml ground ginger
Pinch (1 ml) ground nutmeg
2 teaspoons (10 ml) bicarbonate of soda
4 large, free-range eggs
1 cup (250 ml) light brown sugar
150 grams butter, melted
1 cup (250 ml) buttermilk

Topping:
¼ cup (62.5 ml) double cream
¼ cup (62.5 ml) butter, melted
1 cup (250 ml) brown sugar
¼ cup (62.5 ml) desiccated coconut
¼ cup (62.5 ml) flaked almonds/ chopped nuts of your choice

Directions

- Preheat the oven to 165°C and prepare a silicone mold or medium sized cake tin by rubbing with butter or spraying with cooking spray
- Sift together the dry ingredients
- Whisk the eggs in a separate bowl and gradually add the sugar until light and fluffy
- Add the butter and buttermilk
- Add to the dry ingredients and mix until smooth
- Pour into the cake tin/ mold and bake for around 45 minutes until cooked
- Cool and turn out
- Mix the ingredients for the topping and spread over the cake
- Place in oven and grill/ bake until golden brown
- Cool and serve

BANANA BREAD

Ingredients

2 cups (500 ml) plain flour
1 teaspoon (5 ml) baking powder
Pinch (1 ml) ground pink salt
½ cup (125 ml) butter
¾ cup (187.5 ml) brown sugar
2 large, free-range eggs, beaten
5 ripe bananas, mashed with a fork

Directions

- Preheat the oven to 165°C (180°C if not a convection fan oven)
- Combine the dry ingredients (flour, salt, baking powder)
- Whisk together the butter and sugar until light in colour
- Add the eggs and bananas to the flour mixture
- Transfer to a prepared loaf tin and bake for approximately 60 minutes or until a skewer placed into the centre of the loaf comes out clean

BAKED APPLE PUDDING

THIS IS ONE OF MY FAVOURITE INDULGENT PUDDINGS (BECAUSE IT CONTAINS CREAM AND QUITE A BIT OF SUGAR). It is also a recipe from my mother's side of the family and made by my mother's sister. Interestingly, she has very similar handwriting to my mother and this is her hand-written recipe that I am sharing below.

Ingredients

1 cup (250 ml) self raising flour
1 cup (250 ml) castor sugar
3 large apples, cut into slices and cooked
3 tablespoons (45 ml) melted butter
2 large, free-range eggs
¼ cup (62.5 ml) semi-skimmed milk
Pinch (1 ml) of ground pink salt

Directions

- Preheat the oven to 165°C (180°C if not a convection fan oven)
- Whisk the eggs and sugar until light and creamy
- Add the milk and butter
- Gradually add the flour and mix well
- Pour into a pre-treated baking dish (lined/ treated with butter or cooking spray)
- Spread the apples out evenly and bake for around 30 - 45 minutes

SAUCE

Ingredients

1 cup (250 ml) sugar
¾ cup (187.5 ml) cream
1 teaspoon (5 ml) vanilla or orange extract

Directions

- Heat together and pour over the pudding as soon as it comes out of the oven

MALVA PUDDING

IF YOU COULD BOTTLE MEMORIES OF YOUR CHILDHOOD, THIS ONE WILL ALWAYS REMIND ME OF MY MOTHER'S FAMILY IN CAPE TOWN.

The French descent is clearly visible in their features – same lovely hands, wide, small feet and those clear, sapphire eyes.

All I know is that French descent or not, they love a good braai, making potjies and eating together.

Going for visits from Namibia and then eventually studying and working in Cape Town, I am blessed to have gotten to know them better and spend time with them over the years.

This pudding made by my mother's youngest sister is a regular feature at these family gatherings (as is my mother's other sister's apple pudding).

Ingredients

1 large, free-range egg
½ cup (125 ml) castor sugar
1 cup (250 ml) plain flour
1.5 tablespoons (22.5 ml) white vinegar
1 tablespoon (15 ml) apricot jam
1 teaspoon (5 ml) baking powder
1 teaspoon (5 ml) bicarbonate of soda
1 cup (250 ml) semi-skimmed milk
Pinch (1 ml) of ground pink salt

Directions

- Preheat the oven to 165°C (180°C if not a convection fan oven)
- Whisk together the egg and sugar until light in colour
- Add the dry ingredients (flour, baking powder, bicarbonate of soda)
- Add the vinegar, jam, milk and salt and mix thoroughly
- Transfer to pre-treated baking dish (lined or treated with butter or cooking spray) and bake for approximately 60 minutes (in my oven it is cooked after 25 minutes so check it after 30 minutes at the most)

SAUCE

Ingredients

1 cup (250 ml) sugar
1 cup (250 ml) semi-skimmed milk
½ cup (125 ml) hot water
125 grams butter
1 teaspoon (5 ml) vanilla extract/ bean paste

Directions

- Heat together all the ingredients and pour over the sponge as soon as you take it from the oven
- Serve hot or cold with custard, cream, ice cream or on its own

VOLUME TWO:
HERITAGE

IF I COULD WRITE A NOTE TO MYSELF WHEN I STARTED THIS BOOK, I MIGHT HAVE SAID SOMETHING LIKE

My Dearest M,

You have the hazelnut eyes and short nail, sensitive hands of your dad; the fine, wavy hair and small, wide feet of your mom.

You have their dimples, freckles, ears, nose and chin. You share their passion, humour and stubbornness within.

Yes, you are the curves of decades of family instilled by your grandmother; the traditions of church, Sunday lunch, Easter, Christmas and New Year.

You have experienced loss, pain, years of challenges and have a history of sorrow. Yet you regurgitate their hard work, grit and love, so why do you fear tomorrow?

I would probably smile, thinking back to the time when I had to write an actual essay entitled "I am..." for school aged around 17.

How hard it felt for me at the time, how adamant my English teacher was that I should be a writer rather than the scientist I had always envisioned.

How surprisingly hard it still is now many years later when I do mostly write for a living to try and unwrap myself from my baking; still searching for the right words to use to say just how much I feel and care.

In part I guess it goes back to sharing a fundamental heritage with people who care deeply, but where it was (and is) not OK to talk about your feelings or show pain.

A people who had to be strong and naturally competitive with mostly predefined roles of what it meant to be fathers or wives or children (who should be seen and not heard).

How you dared not disrespect your elders and, as my mother would remind me constantly, "turn the other cheek and walk away" when someone behaved rudely or hurt you.

Looking back, I wonder if my father was still alive if he could ever tell me how he felt the day my grandfather died before his eyes, what went on in his heart when his first child was born or when he finally had the son he always wanted.

I wonder how he felt when he lay there in the hospital bed struggling to breathe after a heart attack. Whether he would take back his comment about being OK, that he only needed to be at home for three months before he was better; instead choosing to tell my sisters that he loved them before he took his last breath.

I wonder if he would read this, if he would be proud of our own survival in a far distant land.

I would never know, because we did not talk about pain or feelings or for that matter love.

But to heal and move on after loss, we do have to talk.

Because baking, like life and finding lasting love, is a process. One you need to follow and go through to taste the reward.

Fortunately, I did get to talk to my grandmother from time to time. We spoke about baking, the incredible pain of childbirth, breastfeeding and loss of loved ones.

These conversations sadly did not happen often; being on the other side of the world would do that. They do remind me though that despite of her tough exterior, my grandmother was, like me, just human.

She cared deeply, always making time to talk.

She would always ask me "Now tell me Marianna..." keen to find out what everyone else was up to, when last I heard of so and so, how the kids were doing at school, etc., etc.

It reminds me that heritage is fundamental to who and what we are. Being human however means we might fail while we learn, thereby creating a better reality for ourselves and our loved ones in the future.

So, although my mother does not bake and would probably never really understand why I do, I keep working on having meaningful conversations with her.

Conversations about love and loss, dreams and challenges.

She cannot solve my challenges. Yet she listens, does not judge, say she will pray for me and rejoices in my joy.

I have the fine, wavy hair of my mom, the hazelnut eyes of my dad.

Mostly though I am me, navigating a way through life with my baking as therapy.

Writing a new page on my journey to inner peace, knowing that despite not really being understood, I am very much loved.

MELKTERT

THERE ARE MANY VARIATIONS FOR MELKTERT AND IT REALLY SEEMS TO STEM FROM HOW YOU LIKE YOUR TART CASE (SHE SAYS TRYING NOT TO GIGGLE).

Whether puffed, short crust or none, Melktert is quite similar in taste to custard tarts or casa de natas.

It is however through and through a South African favourite and not intended to be yellow in colour or caramelised on the top.

This is my grandmother's recipe and is enough for five Melkterts.

The pastry can be chilled or frozen and used when needed. I prefer to eat this chilled, but you can warm it in the oven to reach room temperature.

Ingredients

Tart case:
2 cups (500 ml) plain flour
2 teaspoons (10 ml) baking powder
1 teaspoon (5 ml) ground pink salt
2 large, free-range eggs
¼ cup (62.5 ml) margarine or butter
½ cup (125 ml) sugar

Tart filling:
9 cups (2.25 litres) semi-skimmed milk
6 tablespoons (90 ml) butter
4 large eggs, separated (whites beaten to stiff peak stage)
5 tablespoons (75 ml) plain flour
5 tablespoons (75 ml) corn flour
1.5 cups (375 ml) sugar
½ teaspoon (2.5 ml) ground pink salt
2 teaspoons (10 ml) vanilla essence/ bean paste

Directions

Tart case:

- Preheat the oven to 145°C (165°C if not convection fan oven)
- Use your fingers and rub flour, baking powder, salt, sugar and butter together until resembling fine crumbs
- Add the beaten eggs and mix
- Divide into five and use pastry to line five pie/ tart cases
- Blind bake until light brown – around 10 minutes

Tart filling:

- Add the ingredients together and heat in a pan
- Fold in the egg whites (do this quickly)
- Pour into cases and sprinkle over some cinnamon/ nutmeg
- Bake at around 145°C for around 25 minutes until set

These are best served immediately or kept in a fridge or chiller

KOEKSISTERS

I HAVE OFTEN WONDERED IF THE PERSON(S) WHO INVENTED KOEKSISTERS EVER THOUGHT ABOUT THE SYMBOLISM OF THOSE SWEET AND INTOXICATING PIECES OF INTERTWINED DOUGH.

How the mere act of plaiting or twisting those many strands before you fry them in hot oil can move you to a place of complete nostalgia or trigger sensual memory.

Apparently "koek" is the Dutch word for "cake". No surprise there haha. There is also a story told about sisters who plaited their doughnuts before dunking these into syrup.

Koeksisters remind me not only of school and church bazaars (fairs/ fêtes) where money was usually raised, but of what could have been, what might still be.

A reminder now of how two lives can intertwine easily or intricately and come apart just as easily, if not attached together in the right way from the start.

Admittedly, finding the right someone to intertwine your life with in the first place can be complicated. After making koeksisters the first time after my separation, I wrote:

In that moment and in that time, our souls touched
and like muscles they remembered
(as they embraced one another
...slowly at first)
Every curve and perfect imperfection
And as they let go, I let you go
Because time (and for now us) belonged to someone else

However you make your koeksisters (this is my grandmother's recipe), remember to give yourself ample time to cut and prepare the dough. Enjoy the process, feel the dough between your fingers as you plait or twist and remember it is OK to feel every type of emotion when you bake. Happy plaiting.

KOEKSISTERS DOUGH

Ingredients

6 cups (1.5 litres) plain flour
4 teaspoons (20 ml) baking powder
1 teaspoon (5ml) ground pink salt
3 large, free-range eggs
3 tablespoons (45 ml) butter
400 ml semi-skimmed milk

Directions

- Sift together the dry ingredients (flour, salt, baking powder)
- Rub the butter in with your fingers
- Add the beaten eggs and milk
- Knead together until mixed thoroughly
- Cover and leave at least 3 hours or overnight
- Roll the dough until it is around 3mm (1/8 inch) thick
- Plait loosely
- Bake in hot oil
- Dunk into syrup immediately, remove and place onto cooling rack

SYRUP:

Ingredients

10 cups (2.5 litres) of sugar
3 tablespoons (45 ml) lemon juice
2 teaspoons (10 ml) cream of tartar
Piece of fresh ginger
6 cups (1.5 litres) water
3 tablespoons (45 ml) golden syrup
1 teaspoon (5 ml) glycerin

Directions

- Dissolve the sugar in the water while stirring
- Add lemon juice when syrup starts to boil
- Cook for 5 minutes
- Add the golden syrup, glycerin and cream or tartare
- Pour through sieve and chill until very cold

CAPE BRANDY PUDDING (TIPSY TART)

BRANDY IS A SERIOUSLY SOUTH AFRICAN THING.

In fact, mixed with a popular brand of cola, it is about as synonymous with braaing (what some people would mistakenly call a BBQ) as boerewors (mostly beef sausage). I would be in serious trouble for even suggesting it is used to refer to the same thing.

Up to now I have not fully developed a taste for brandy.

It might have something to do with the fact that I think of my mom burning out the alcohol in a tablespoon before making me swallow the brandy as medicine. Usually when I had an upset tummy - lovely...not!

Cognac has not made me like it any more either... it just amplifies those aromas and memories of tummy upsets. Sorry to disappoint.

Nevertheless, I used to measure the ingredients for Tipsy Tart every Friday at a popular family eatery where I got my first part-time job. Fortunately, the brandy was already pre-measured and sealed.

It is the smell of the brandy syrup (the alcohol mostly evaporates) that brings back those memories of being in that store room, pulling together flour, dates, nuts, sugar, etc. for the ladies working in the kitchen to bake, together with baked cheesecake and a very popular health loaf from a certain Salad Valley.

I enjoy serving this pudding with thick, chilled custard. It keeps for days in the fridge (it has quite a bit of brandy to preserve it after all) and is also suitable for freezing.

Ingredients

Sponge base:

250 grams dates, chopped and stones removed
1 teaspoon (5 ml) bicarbonate of soda
1 cup (250 ml) hot water
125 grams butter or margarine
¾ cup (187.5 ml) castor sugar
3 large, free-range eggs
1.5 cups (375 ml) plain flour
2 teaspoons (10 ml) baking powder
½ teaspoon (2.5 ml) ground ginger
Pinch of ground pink salt
50 grams pecan/ hazel nuts, chopped

Syrup:

1 cup (250 ml) sugar
1 cup (250 ml) hot water
1 tablespoon (15 ml) butter
½ teaspoon (2.5 ml) ground cinnamon
¼ to ½ cup (62.5 ml - 125 ml) brandy
1 teaspoon (5 ml) vanilla essence/ extract/ bean paste

Directions

- Preheat oven to 165°C (180°C if not a convection fan oven)
- Prepare (line or treat with margarine or butter or cooking spray) a medium-sized pie dish
- Mix the dates, bicarbonate of soda and hot water and leave for 5 minutes
- Cream the butter and sugar together until light and fluffy
- Add the eggs one at a time and mix
- Sift the dry ingredients and mix together with the egg and butter mixture
- Add the dates and nuts (this makes me giggle) and fold in gently
- Transfer to the pie dish and bake for approximately 60 minutes until cooked
- While the pudding is baking, mix the sugar, boiling water, butter and cinnamon in a pan and stir on a gentle heat until the sugar is dissolved
- Simmer for a few minutes, remove from heat, add the brandy and vanilla essence
- Skewer pudding and pour over the sauce. Leave to absorb. Serve

BREAD (BROOD)

FARM LOAF

Ingredients

1 kg bread or plain flour
10 grams instant yeast
2 tablespoons (30 ml) rapeseed/ sunflower/ olive oil
2 tablespoons (30 ml) white vinegar
2 teaspoons (10 ml) sugar
600 ml lukewarm water

Directions

- Preheat oven to around 165°C (180°C if not a convection fan oven)
- Sift together the dry ingredients
- Combine the oil and water and then mix with the dry ingredients
- Knead until soft and elastic and no longer sticking to your hands (around 10 minutes)
- Cover and let the dough rise for 2-3 hours or until double in size
- Knead for a couple of minutes – the dough will collapse as soon as you touch it
- Divide and transfer into bread pans/ similar. Let it rise again until double in size
- Bake for around 1 hour or until cooked (skewer inserted into the middle comes out clean)

YOGHURT LOAF

Ingredients

3.5 cups (875 ml) whole-wheat flour
2 teaspoons (10 ml) baking powder
¼ cup (62.5 ml) semi-skimmed milk
2 cups (500 ml) plain Greek style yoghurt
½ teaspoon (2.5 ml) honey
Pinch of ground pink salt

Directions

- Preheat oven to around 165°C (180°C if not a convection fan oven)
- Mix ingredients and transfer to a pre-prepared loaf tin
- Bake for around 60 minutes until cooked
- Cool down and turn out

VETKOEK

For thousands of Southern Africans around the world vetkoek is a true taste of home.

Served with curry or simply with butter and jam, you can easily be forgiven for not wanting to stop eating once you have started.

Being able to make vetkoek though is a real skill.

Once you have read the recipe, you might say surely it is just fried bread… Not so.

Vetkoek is a test.

Those who can use a light touch and demonstrate some patience, will win every time. But like everything, a little practice is usually all that is needed.

My vetkoek memories are of whole-meal vetkoek, left to rise under a blanket in the sun. My mother's small hands kneading them off before frying them in hot oil.

Every now and then we would be allowed to help her knead the dough.

Mostly we would be carrying the big enamel bowl to and from the wall to rise or bring inside.

When you make this, you will understand that this dough is like a baby – it needs gently looking after. Also, as it is a double rise method, it is worth taking your time. This is not something you would want to redo.

Ingredients

1 kg white bread flour (or half whole-wheat, half white)
1.5 teaspoons (7 ml) sugar
2 ml ground pink salt
10 grams dried, instant yeast
2 – 2.5 cups (500 ml – 600 ml) lukewarm water

Directions

- Mix the dry ingredients
- Add just enough water to form a malleable dough (not sticking to your fingers)
- Knead until soft and elastic (10-15 minutes)
- Cover with cling film/ similar and leave to rise until double in volume
- Knead off and roll out on a floured surface until 2-3 centimetres in thickness
- Cut into squares
- Fry in hot oil until puffed up and brown
- Enjoy with filling or topping of your choice

PLAATKOEKIES

Ingredients

2 large, free-range eggs
½ cup (125 ml) castor sugar
1 cup (250 ml) semi-skimmed milk
2 tablespoons (30 ml) margarine or butter, melted
2 cups (500 ml) plain flour
4 teaspoons (20 ml) baking powder
½ teaspoon (5ml) ground pink salt

Directions

- Whisk together the eggs and sugar until light in colour
- Add the milk and the margarine or butter
- Sift together the dry ingredients and add to the mixture
- Take one tablespoon of batter at a time and drop into a pan with oil (medium heat)
- Turn over when golden at the bottom and fry until cooked through
- Serve with golden syrup or honey or a topping of your choice

ALL-PURPOSE PASTRY

This recipe is brilliant for using left-over roasts, etc. My grandmother shared this with me one Boxing (family) Day after I complained about having so much duck left over from the Christmas roast.

It is super quick and easy and a definite winner in my opinion.

Ingredients

2.5 cups (625 ml) plain flour
200 ml sunflower oil
200 ml hot water

Directions

- Preheat oven to 165°C (180°C if not a convection fan oven)
- Shake ingredients together in bottle, then add over pie ingredients of your choice
- Bake for around 20-40 minutes

SAVOURY MUFFINS

THIS RECIPE IS WHAT I CALL A PERFECT FILLER.

The kind of recipe everyone needs when you must bake comfort food without the luxury of time or lots of experience. You can change the vegetables according to what you have available and choose your favourite cheese. It really is quick and easy and delivers tasty bites in around 30 minutes.

Ingredients

1.5 cups (375 ml) self raising flour
2 cups (500 ml) grated cheese of your choice
100 grams salami/ viennas cut into pieces
1 zucchini/ baby marrow grated
¼ cup (62.5 ml) chives, finely cut
¾ cup (180 ml) semi-skimmed milk
1 large, free-range egg
¼ cup (62.5 ml) chutney (I make my own apple chutney)

Directions

- Preheat the oven to 165°C (180°C if not a convection fan oven)
- Grease/ spray a muffin pan
- Sift flour
- Add cheese, meat, zucchini and chives
- Whisk milk, egg and chutney and add to the dry mixture and mix
- Spoon into a muffin pan
- Bake for 20 – 25 minutes until skewer inserted into the centre comes out clean
- Rest for a few minutes and turn out

CHEMISTRY

If I poured a single drop of what I feel into what I bake
would you taste the bittersweet of being in love,
feel the pain of lost love
or just think 'yes, that is some good baking'?

THE TRUTH FOR ME IS THAT I LOVE TO BAKE AND BAKE TO REMIND MYSELF OF HOW TO LOVE.

To love openly and freely, reminding myself not to be afraid of trying new things or failing.

The ability to express myself honestly and with passion. Give because I can and because I care.

But like so many who have been hurt, I realise that I had become scared of the very thing that I treasure the most.

When my marriage eventually ended, it was not because of some sordid affair or because we got married to soon.

Over the years our love withered away because we stopped doing the very things a lasting relationship needs most – communicating openly and working as a team.

Our dreams of a better life in Wales and spending quality time together as a family died because we put other people's feelings and needs before our own.

So instead of building each other up, we started tearing each other down through little acts of passive resistance and non-cooperation.

Over time, my sense of loss and loneliness felt so great that to cope I stopped myself from feeling anything at all that was not related to the kids or my customers.

I stopped myself from expressing the very feelings and words I needed to say to get through this.

I buried that girl with curves and hopes and dreams under layers of black, work and more work.

When I eventually came face-to-face with my feelings of stress and anxiety, I realised that the very support structure I thought I could rely on, did not exist.

I had to choose, get out or leave who I was to disappear forever.

CLEMENTINE DRIZZLE CAKE

> *"Have we met before?"*

> *"No, but we have friends in common"*

> *"Only 2"*

PRECISION AND ACCURACY... Two qualities I really admire. So, if you want precision and accuracy, it might be worth looking away now.

My baking is very much a reflection of me – balance, but not precision. It certainly is more about the proportions, texture and taste than about ingredients measured exactly.

So how do you reconcile a desire for precision with a desire for passion? You learn to let go and trust and listen to your instincts. For me this cake is a perfect example of that.

A combination of simple accuracy with amazing sensuality. The kind of cake that seduces even the baker with its volume, flavour and natural beauty.

This is a cake that tastes like cheesecake, but rises like a souffle and lasts for days. Possibly the only cake I immediately want another slice of.

Ingredients

5 large, free-range eggs, separated
1 cup (250 ml) castor sugar
Zest and juice of 3 clementines
225 grams butter, melted
1 cup (250 ml) plain flour, sifted
3 teaspoons (15 ml) baking powder

Syrup:
¼ cup (62.5 ml) clementine juice
¼ cup (62.5 ml) sugar
2 tablespoons (30 ml) orange liqueur

Directions

- Preheat the oven to 165°C (180°C if not a convection fan oven) and prepare a medium cake tin with butter or cooking spray
- Whisk together the egg yolks and sugar until light and thick
- Add the orange juice, zest and melted butter
- Add the sifted flour and baking powder
- Whisk the egg whites until stiff peak stage (eggs for stiff peaks that do not collapse when the whisk is removed)
- Add the mixture and pour into baking tin
- Bake for 35-40 minutes until golden and cooked (skewer inserted into the centre comes out clean)
- Heat together the remaining orange juice and sugar until the sugar has melted. Add the orange liqueur
- Remove the cake from the oven. Pierce with a skewer and pour over the syrup
- Let cool and turn out
- Dust with icing sugar or mix icing sugar and orange juice and drizzle over top

CARROT CAKE

What do you say about a cake that by its very nature says fruity...

Of course, unless you add pineapple, carrot cake is more carrot than anything else, but you do of course add raisins or sultanas, etc.

Still to this day there are not that many cakes from Southern Africa that uses a vegetable as its main ingredient, especially with oil instead of butter and no milk.

For me, carrot cake is heavenly.

The look, the taste and especially the cream cheese icing.

In fact, sometimes I think it really is the combination of creamy sour and cinnamon that I crave, rather than the cake itself.

Nevertheless, carrot cake is a keeper.

One of those cakes that lasts, only I suggest that you ice it just before you plan to serve it or keep it chilled once you've iced it.

Just remember, chilling a cake changes its taste.

Ingredients

4 large, free-range eggs
1.5 cups (375 ml) sugar
1 cup (250 ml) sunflower oil
3 cups (750 ml) grated carrots
1 cup (250 ml) tinned pineapple, mashed
2.5 cups (625 ml) plain flour
1.25 teaspoons (7.5 ml) baking powder
1 teaspoon (5 ml) bicarbonate of soda
1.25 teaspoons (7.5 ml) ground cinnamon
1 teaspoon (5 ml) ground pink salt
100 grams chopped nuts of your choice

Directions

- Preheat oven to around 165°C (180°C if not a convection fan oven)
- Prepare two medium sized baking pans/ silicon mold (lined or pre-treated with butter or cooking spray)
- Whisk together the eggs and sugar until light and airy
- Add the oil, carrots and pineapple and stir
- Sift together the dry ingredients (flour, baking powder, bicarbonate of soda, cinnamon and salt)
- Add to the carrot mixture and mix thoroughly
- Transfer to the baking tins/ mold and bake for 60-70 minutes until cooked
- Cool and turn out onto cooling rack
- Decorate with your choice of topping

DRIZZLE ICING

Ingredients

1 cup (250 ml) icing sugar
3 tablespoons (45 ml) orange/ lemon juice

Directions

- Mix together the icing sugar and orange juice
- Spread over the cake

CREAM CHEESE ICING

Ingredients

½ cup (125 ml) cottage cheese
2 cups (500 ml) icing sugar
¼ cup (62.5 ml) butter
1 teaspoon (5 ml) vanilla extract
1 tablespoon (15 ml) grated orange/ lemon/ clementine peel/ zest

Directions

- Mix together the cream cheese and icing sugar little by little
- Whisk until light and smooth
- Add the vanilla extract and zest/ peel
- Spread over the cake and sprinkle over nuts

APPLE CAKE

SURPRISINGLY APPLES ARE NOT THAT COMMON IN SOUTHERN AFRICA.

I am not talking about Granny Smith or Gala apples, of those there are plenty.

I am talking about the dozens of varieties of apples found in the UK and elsewhere that are neither sour or floury that make baking this cake a thorough delight.

Admittedly apples would not be my number one choice of fruit to eat by itself, but when it comes to baking this cake, these handfuls of delights certainly come into their own.

For this recipe I would suggest apples that are not cookers, as these tend to be too tart.

The best thing is there are literally hundreds of varieties, so feel free to experiment.

Ingredients

2 medium sized apples, peeled and grated
Zest of 1 lemon/ clementine/ orange
1 cup (250 ml) castor/ brown sugar
1 cup (250 ml) sunflower oil
1 cup (250 ml) golden syrup
1 teaspoon (5 ml) ground ginger
1 teaspoon (5 ml) ground cinnamon
½ teaspoon (2 ml) ground allspice
3 cups (750 ml) plain flour
2 teaspoons (10 ml) baking powder
1 cup (250 ml) Rooibos or other tea of your choice
2 teaspoons (10 ml) baking powder
1 large, free-range egg, lightly beaten

Directions

- Preheat the oven to 165°C (180°C if not a convection fan oven) and prepare a hollow cake tin with butter or cooking spray
- Mix together the apple and lemon/ clementine/ orange
- Add the spices, sugar, oil and syrup and mix thoroughly
- Sift together the flour and baking powder
- Add the tea and bicarbonate of soda and mix together with the rest of the ingredients
- Pour mixture into the cake tin and bake for approximately 60 minutes until cooked
- Cool and turn out
- Dust with icing sugar and decorate with zest of a lemon/ lime/ clementine

THE NEXT VOLUME:
TO DRINK OR NOT TO DRINK ROOIBOS TEA

No fashion collection worth its salt is ever complete without a signature show stopper.

Baking for many is very much like fashion - what is of the moment, aligned with the latest diet guaranteed to make you lose pounds within weeks, what is made or chosen by which A-list celebrity...

The truth – at least for people like me – is that good design, like good baking, lasts the test of time.

Admittedly, I have never been the biggest admirer of fruit cake – mostly because it gives me heartburn. However, this one reminds me of the one my grandmother used to make for my dad at Christmas.

It is no lightweight and can easily weigh up to 2 kg (approximately 4 pounds), but its taste is beautifully light and fragrant, can be frozen and does not need to be iced.

This is also the cake that I posted to a soldier and dear friend for Christmas and his response has inspired this book.

His thank you message read something like:

> *"When you write your cookbook you can say Polish, American, Australian, UK and South African men like your cooking"*

My reply: "Ha-ha, very funny. Do not see that happening anytime soon."

As you try this cake, remember that baking is real act of self. When you love it like I do, everything you bake has that little added extra – a piece of you.

I can assure you this cake lasts a while provided you do not leave it somewhere too warm – after all its shelf-life was tested by some real-life heroes.

ROOIBOS TEA FRUIHT CAKE

Ingredients

2-3 Rooibos tea bags
1.5 cups (375 ml) hot water
1.25 cups (375 ml) sugar
2 teaspoons (10 ml) bicarbonate of soda
2 cups of self raising flour
1 cup (approximately 100 grams) nuts of your choice
2 large, free-range eggs, lightly beaten
3 cups fruit cake mix of your choice
1 cup (approximately 100 grams) glacé cherries
1/3 cup (83 grams) stem ginger in syrup
125 g butter

Directions

- Preheat the oven to 165°C (180°C if not a convection fan oven)
- Infuse tea for around 5 minutes
- Add fruitcake mix and leave to soak up liquid for a further 5 minutes
- Simmer with the butter and sugar for around 15 minutes
- Add the bicarbonate of soda and leave to cool
- Add the flour, eggs, cherries, ginger and nuts
- Transfer to a medium sized lined or treated cake tin/ mold
- Bake for approximately 60 minutes or until a skewer inserted into the centre of the cake comes out clean
- Cover. This cake can be left for several days before eating it or frozen
- When ready to serve, dust with icing sugar and edible glitter

EPILOGUE

In M's Kitchen I have learnt many lessons over the past few years.

The most important lessons I have learned about baking is that you should trust your instincts and keep practicing.

If it feels right and smells right, it will turn out fine, trust your gut.

What is more, do not be afraid to experiment and adapt recipes to your environment.

Experience makes you brave only because you are prepared to risk something to achieve a desired goal.

The look of appreciation from a loved one and the time spent watching them enjoy my baking is my ultimate reward.

For me baking really is the gift of love and time that will keep on giving. It is also one of the best sources of therapy and healing I have found in a long time.

Until next time